VOTIVE MESS

Nia Davies is a poet experimenting with embodied practice and performance. She was editor of the international journal *Poetry Wales* from 2014 to 2019. Her pamphlets, *Then Spree* (Salt, 2012), *Çekoslovak-yalılaştıramadıklarımızdanmısınız* or *Long Words* (Boiled String, 2016), *England* (Crater, 2017), *Key blank* (LPB, 2018) and several collaborative works, were followed by *All fours* (Bloodaxe Books, 2017), which was shortlisted for the Roland Mathias Poetry Award 2018 (Wales Book of the Year Awards) and longlisted for the 2019 Michael Murphy Memorial Prize for a distinctive first book of poetry. Nia works in interdisciplinary research and completed a doctorate in 2021 on ritual and performance in poetry practice. She co-curated Poetry Emergency festivals in 2018 and 2019 and has worked on intercultural collaborative literary and translation projects around the world. Nia lives in Cymru/Wales. Her second book-length collection, *Votive Mess*, was published by Bloodaxe Books in 2024.

NIA DAVIES

Votive Mess

BLOODAXE BOOKS

ISBN: 978 1 78037 715 5

First published 2024 by
Bloodaxe Books Ltd,
Eastburn,
South Park,
Hexham,
Northumberland NE46 1BS.

www.bloodaxebooks.com
For further information about Bloodaxe titles
please visit our website and join our mailing list
or write to the above address for a catalogue.

Supported using public funding by
**ARTS COUNCIL
ENGLAND**

Cover design: Neil Astley & Pamela Robertson-Pearce.

Printed in Great Britain by Bell & Bain Limited, Glasgow, Scotland, on
acid-free paper sourced from mills with FSC chain of custody certification.

CONTENTS

Ritual Steps, Paviland

Rite – pupils, neck, diaphragm

Rite – breaking open and up, breathing and living adfeilion

Rite – unfinished plethu

Rite – a thread to visit my loves' loves' loves, by night, by ether-frag

Rite – lapse into a new language/ incant-enchant against private wards/
    against death, debt

Rite – for the opposite of alienation, an escape in the likeness of an otter,
an arrival in the likeness of an utter

Rite – a daubing of untitled powder, to hurls to howls to singz, now you
    keep a book on a string

Rite – a social rhythm, for decades. For seconds. For the cuckoo

Rite – the precarity of a breathing cycle, its passage

Rite – a dedication to the dying

Write – you want a change or rest or a continuum

Right – to claim back, to deprivatise our I's

Wright – a tradesperson weaves between me and my loves' loves' loves,
    the redder thread

Rite – act of poesie in a daubing, this ochre ash, the red lad

Rite – and to close is also love, pass something on, something less grave

Rite – gathered, offered, pre-cant, washed away for a future

Rite – the body grateful, the ash redder

Mieri

I was hurting in the brain of the dead.
This was their meaning, their poem.
They had my meaning and I had to inherit it.

That very same night
a valley of shortening,
a charcoal stick to think with,
I sketched loops to survive
the slam of unknown impact.
If only it were Manx shearwater.

I am committing. Meanwhile something,
it doesn't matter what, is for sale. *Cofiwch*,
still furious, water coming towards water.
This branded teatowel tells me of the
dissipation that happens everyday.

And that I have lost what the dead entrusted me with.
And still trying to control lost things,
to name, and rename.

Here I am sinking into habitus
when I could be sinking into the lost things
or the still-losing things. Cofiwch:
y Humedal Antiñir, Puerto Montt,
where the gorse glows
all year round. Like here.
I'll commit to calling myself your girlfriend
when the gorse ceases to flower.
I'll commit to being with you
when I learn enough Cymraeg to read *Adfeilion Babel*

I'll commit to the bramble pits of bomb craters,
commit to lost time & words
which slowly climb up the cervical spine.

I took *Adfeilion Babel* for a face.
The book was an inanimate object
that became animate on my face
and in my spine. So I wear the ruins of Babel
as a mask, bramble pits as ruins in my voice.

Mieri – symbols of agonising
regeneration or green trip wires where, Cofiwch
Mwyara. The blackberries are books
full of juice and I'll commit to you
as brambles when I finish my books.

*

Ni ddylai hiraeth am amgyffred undod iaith yn y gorffennol neu'r dyfodol ein rhwystro
rhag ymhyfrydu yn elfennau amryliw, symudliw patrymau ieithyddol y presennol.

CARYL DAVIES, *Adfeilion Babel*

Communitas / Anti-Communitas / Communitas

Crowds are in the courtyard reasoning with their fingers, clinging to their city, to their sadnesses. Great power is given to their sheep-dog rulers. They hurry to make a cube or a circle, take their shirts off. They're back from ten years in the rubble plots, trained, preponderous and armed in note-taking. They make geological accretions, each person amassing an era, a layer. Later, a crowd on top of that crowd already past. The passing of bodies through a matchbox, their skins traced in occasioned loving, full remembered, full lost. They find mutiny in small ideas. Then the wash of their movement towards the food behind you. You have to wait until they've feasted before you can move, you have to wait until they've moved before you can eat. Their abundance brings several flint knock feelings to the head. Their shirts are flung all this way over you and you are part of them. You are separate, but you are not separate, you are part of them & you are not part of them.

With & for Amrita Shah

Dick Joke Poem

Sometimes the hemlock pushes back in a reflux
and it's all I can do but take pleasure
sometimes I want to breath all over your face my fumes
or shoplift a product to try it before I pay a fool's ransom
and then the closeness of the surveillance haunts me out.

Sometimes such closeness is percolating, like you're
being watched by a mechanical boss and even though I'm
free from that eye briefly, the future holds panoptic possibilities.
Caught in horizon's reflux, a static moment where I held on to
a breathing apparatus to steady, an oxygen cylinder as a pet.

A film where I limped across a stony driveway. Perhaps the dick jokes
aren't all bad and I can be steady with your
quick text. He's boarding a plane to Ahmedabad, she's fixing her sink in
Berlin, a knock at the door and here are Viennese whirls in
a ziplock bag, what did you get your Mam in the end, I
got her a balancing ball, under a tenner in Aldi.

The question about the nature of the hemlock doesn't go away.
I dream my bike breaks on my way to Newfield school where
I have gone back to work as a support assistant and I'm
late and the broken bike gets stolen on Carterknowle road,
which is the wrong side of the hill. A classic
angst dream with interesting backflash to
'oh it's so sweet you want to volunteer for us',

when I had thought this was a paid job. Some figment
of humiliation and precarity, some leavetaking.
But the surveillance is heavier now and
I'm better at stretching, and men and women and poetry, actually maybe not
poems, will never understand the old mercury. Blessed too are my
sexual fantasies which are far more elaborate.

The patients, we must presume, never leave
the desert retreat for hypersensitivity, Wrenwood
and what made you sick? Remember you made you sick, oh yes.
That was 1993, *Safe*, with Julianne Moore.

I keep this charm safe next to my bra I didn't lift it from Aldi,
they won't find me to advertise eye cream to me.
Sometimes the hemlock represents mercurial potion, half
killing half joy. Unpicking its appearance in one's mind
is like picking at the scab in the navel of the dream.
Why was I riding a bike to the school/workplace
on the other side of a steep vale.
Hemlock is the martyrdom of philosophy, the apogee.
It sounds like headlock, see this cod analysis.
Enveloped by fumes in the dry cleaner's,
Julianne Moore has a seizure. Of a sudden she's

a white rod in fish pose on the floor,
red spots bursting on her creamy impeccables,
we're not sure if it's all in her head but I feel those fumes too,
killing hemlock; people speeding up my road, grins out,
cars waiting engines on, pumping,
me too, lifts back and forth across the city.
Poor Julianne moves into a porcelain cave.

Even the desert isn't clean enough. Her oxygen tank gives
her joy, and a further frailty. I'm allergic to you ziplock plastic bag
but I like these biscuits you contained.
Before this, the poem had a figment of the sociocultural,

something of my desires since the age of around 14. Something
about difference and posh people and not so posh people.
It clustered around the words sociocultural/economic.
It had a sad feeling, that of a poem becoming a poem about poetry,
as in poetics. And now I want to leave

you with Julianne Moore's complexion, its transfiguration from glow;
the kind of angelic substance of painters, to lesions and
sunken raw red tissue, still pale despite the red. How her sociocultural
band loosens as the illness provides new identity, subjecthood. She
limps back from her husband's shirt, toxic, and my poem is over.

I Have Taken Many Forms Before I Took This One

Bum yn lliaws rith
Kyn bum kisgyfrith
TALIESIN

1

I like language; I speak then it's true
I love languages, I do not speak, like
I do not speak love
To speak love and language is a like
I like means I love in this language
I do not speak love without these languages as
I love you sweet woman and man
I do not speak my mamiaith so I fetish it
I speak this language unstable, I fetish it

Not knowing the language of my glitchy start, I could know
Mamaiaith (derived from Mamiaith but +a)
Mama+tongue=a a a a   â

How about it then, sweet liking and speaking I love this form
language takes of feeling,
feeling languages extravagantly I stepped out to flawedness
floored by a language I love but cannot speak
though the body speaks it, my language
that is also yours, which we do not speak,
so we smash ourselves *symudliw* against our mixed glitch

Then feeling the speaking body, I stretched out in a language,
this production of the day which occurs each day
getting out of bed to speak language and flawedness
or speaking flaws in my language or my not-lang
my tongue flawless, out of the mouth
where does it sit, iaith neu dafod?

neu bratiaith, where does
my not-lang a   a â a sit, lang-not,
before mouth or between breasts?
Constricted tongue
I mean, it was a joke, but still,

The folds and tricks of saesneg,
its place alongside a   a   a   â. a in the torso.
It is not enough to fold the not-lang a   a   â   into English
It is not enough but it has to be, in the love language
Not saesneg a trellis in the body by which the veins the trees

Liking languages ornately I linked them into me
The trellis that is
A vine which winds through us
an â they cannot take and sell back to us

my not-lang â was so high up in the trellis it was airy
remaining fantastic I grasped it shredding it
little pieces floated down

and I found them among the unstable structure, also a wood
with many other trees
A trellis for the present day
I woke up in a present day and it had to be a production
The language was low growl in an altered tongue
Below an a â a it hurt in the production
of not-language, an altered silence

Maybe it would be best to stay silent
afterall, in such woods as these, a battle of trees.
Those that go out into present day with their language hanging
Do I envy them?

Unstable undecided untranslatable not-lang
Language was the wood we could live in
But in the fray it lost its detail, now it hooks into my trellis
monocultural. Was it the battle inside
the production of the day,
that made this unstable production?
Did we erase a sheen on the brow of our poets?

They say yes. What should we do
today, stretched out in the woods
of our not-lang? Just activities to forget, or fantasies:
I love you sweet person or person of fantastical language
Sweet in one language unstable, one language stretching

Always unstable the stable where the boy was
Sweet swap of silence for not-language
Sweet watch strap, or taste of Turkish Delight in Swydd Efrog

To distract me from the morphing my language takes deeply
my form took the form of the form of the boy.
When-where he was not born of stable but of female liquid
sweet shining brow sweet tree axe
etc. It was a myth they hung their heads on

a trellis, a fungi,   an   a   a â a garden for
stretching and lingual pleasure.
In the domain of Swydd Efrog Delight I told them
we need talk of Taliesin
and he, sweet watch strap, all he wore was shining
sweet brow, sweet mother glitch origin
more acrid than Elmet blacksmith
cauldron spilling language and not-language.
You could've chosen to stay silent sweet man!

In the production of the Celtic twilight in the present day,
Celtic smashed me against the royal language.
And against a royal bridge I smashed my language back,
it smelt so Celtic. But also of Turkish Delight
and beneath that onion.

I needed to produce the present day
not the Celtic Twilight. He said so in his not-language and I
responded wholly, smashed together all this
in delight, what Celtic Delight tastes of in the cauldron
What formed in the torso an a

<pre>
        a a â a   a   a   a â
           â   â   a
              a   â
</pre>

Anti-poetics, anti-techniques

Ritual Poetry: anti-techniques

- Disobedience
- Symudliw (Davies) Treiglo
- The refusal to labour the job beyond the pay
- Bad-square-cosmic-dalliance
- Yeh so 'who of duck's bone had made her needle-case' (Jones).
- Each space in a tiny ficto-critical how the fuck

Poetry as escape, ritual as escape, everything orange, at least for one

Theatres of the mouth

in the body, a corona swaying
have mercy on my phonemes
and check where the tongue is
when reading, writing
you press the palate
tongue down, that's experience
tongue up, that's engagement

tongue to the top-back enamel
that's where pleasure expresses
three emotions in the front mouth
three in the back
and the middle of the mouth is neutral

there's a mathematical formula for this
it makes a rhythm,
on the half beat, your partner might come in
but with a regular beat, means you're no longer in love

and how do we get to pleasure?
Or to the four pleasures to be precise?
The body reading the other body,
then comes eye contact
but, remember gender comes in, we're conditioned, I'm afraid.

There's desire too. Between the three emotions: anger, sadness, happiness
and eight more emotions
and there are really only eight stories too.

Laughter in the belly, it cleanses the organs,
when was the last time?
Anatomy prompts emotions.
When did you cry with tears last?
That's not right, yes, it could be dehydration, but

which sad face is convincing?
stop here, pause, this.

How do actors sustain it? Stamina, yes,
but it's before stamina, leaning back, I say,
this isn't good poetry, I pick up your notebook
you won't react yet, you're conditioned
not to show anger, so when you walk away…

try breathing out with the tongue like that
can you feel the heat? in the cheeks? Or in the stomach,
do you feel neutral?

Feeling the curve around the table too.
Or there's an envelope of mosquito net, or
hey, you seem interesting, i er e i / nt r st ng
interesting, there's no gap for a response
No, it's not in your accent.
Do you feel neutral?

Scores for Ritual Poetry

1. Funeral Games of the Great Mammalia – (David Jones) or, Birth Games of the Little Mamalia
2. Electrics and Water – oil and water, folded together but not dissolving into
3. 'Many Forms Before I was Taken in this One' (Bum yn lliaws rith/ Kyn bum kisgyfrith)
4. The sludgy treatment
5. Mouth placemaking
6. Narcotic Properties (Maggie O'Sullivan)
7. Mask-play, costume-play
8. Expanded verb action texts – timed.
9. Gwers Cymraeg (through estrangement. Feel that it is a comfort to hear it and that tells me I am estranged. That tells me of grief, bureaucratic shell iaith. Rather, I want to dissolve not fold inside, cariad lang)
10. Fold into sludge – a baggy relationship
11. Learn some vocab, repeat repeat repeat
12. Vespers felt fluttering, a chime or a beat that sounded fantastical.
13. Sôn am: placemaking in the word, is it possible?
14. Climb into or onto   (Iaith/Langue/язык/тел)
15. Unmask the imperialist held here within
16. Plough the mouth as a syllable, as a ploughed field to roll around in, mangel-wurzels every arm-length
17. Family dinner: I impressed his family with the joke about the arm of the suitor made of profiteroles. Roll in the mangel-wurzels of a field and leave to chew through the winter
18. Lean dark weeks of action under the cover of gloom, repeat repeat repeat.
19. Cycles of action. Cycles of verbs.
20. Ritual Object on a Scholar's Desk: Rouge Angelique lipstick, by Chanel
21. The copse, the copse. Sex continuous

Multi/direction Bio/poetics

What I desired was to join the historic cult of poet-lovers. I would welcome any emperor the tarot foretold. Em*pourer* who comes unelected, who comes as my equal and ruler.

Arcane in saliva, your oils are already food for my lungs and I would breathe in your discourse. You can all come and touch my solar plexus.

I tried keeping a film of many eyes, many gazes. Kept his smell on the pillow for three days. After the second it went stale. Some licked ears, others anus. Their differing Lacania. I would keep record of a person's constituent auras and vibrations.

But one cannot idealise difference forever before, well, difference. I overboiled with interaction. Laid down. One held my cheeks for years.

You've troubled this conversation into being, I thought, you've taken a beer blonde with my thigh. Can I slit the black cloth we're all sitting on?

I had strayed into a mania of teeth. Also, a theatre of fluids. Theatre of intersecting narcissisms, poet juice, Bollywood yearning. The saints, my friends, billowing. Their discourse settling in the back of my action.

I tried to answer truthfully the questions they asked me but the voices rang out in their special timbres all container, no content. I tried to let myself contract. Now I lie in a darkened room to become less stimulated.

The word I learnt on this day was 'Scotchie'. So I thought of scotch tape sticky at our borders. Hey, come to the borderlands with me, a friend said.

I corresponded with this ruby counsel who took it to heart. Remembered the word 'metrosexual'. I anointed my bed to change its marital status. The reading rooms glowed with wheat and soil colours.

He asked to be smacked expecting I would choose the right side, but I took the left. I worry that was the wrong hand. Are you ready? The way to take poetry seriously is you can all come and pull up my cervical spine.

I've noted my flaws they are hollows in my attention. And when asked, I visualised the multitasking demon, its shaky head and gripping claws. Then, later, the disintegrating owl demon, its grey feather dandruff. There is also the one who cannot give love, it pulls down in a glaucous streak through the organs, hampers the stomach. These all have their constituent allies ready to pull us back up in an upwards motion.

But you need to be ready to be pulled up like that. You need to spell some aura of hello helô. Some of these bus journeys are not appropriate for filing invoices, answering emails. Sometimes men read your love letters over your elbows. Others ask you what you are writing because it is so unusual to see a person writing letters on to paper. Or even reading; a man approached me at the carousel to tell me he loved the fact I was reading a book and not a phone like everyone else and I'm staying at the Hotel Trident.

Other men have cared. Other men were 'splaining but I love my father too much to tell them to go. Others yet say they have a scotchie which means they have a woman they have marked as theirs somehow. I still don't understand the meaning of Scotchie.

Which of your demons or allies flushed up to the surface of this spell? Dearest, history bleeds through the colour of our lips. I wondered if I should feel all the unfelt shame of the ones who had come from my place before me. Or perhaps it's not possible to carry someone else's unfelt shame. Just the demons wriggling underneath. My love, the worst demon is the one who doesn't love at all. Its colour is slate.

Sites / drysfa

where things happened / you do not want to know
three months of not knowing / then flashes / at the site of what
intimate flying / something happened between great tensive denials
and the softness also we felt / some crystals dislodged in the inner ear
who has been cleared out of here / who paid / history audible
then every acceleration / flurried nausea / *lle* neu *man*
into the bluest anthropoi sky then / we / entered a membranous labyrinth
or a bony labyrinth / drysni / which was the particular site
of my dislodging / I asked we / who wants to know what happened

The phenomenology of cut-up

What is phenomenology?
Damp air/
mortar

      Downstairs the drying clothes I worry the damp is caught in the room
                                          must be released
                                                I can smell
                                  I can feel it coming on
                                          coinging on

All of which reveals the true meaning of the
glintzy
    snorting

                              A sequinned outbreath humped sensual
                                    pleasure seeker
                      push back the now in a pleasure-meaning
                      push back the admin in a glintz of break
                    like a horse like a man imitating a horse

Even if this were the case there would still be a need to understand the
                                            anemone
                  We touched their softest maroon pudding bodies
                          attached to multiple crevices
              that was today at Limeslade when I should have been admining
                            that was today touching
                                      sighting
                                    scrying
                  crying; I just want to be outside all the time!

It tries to give a direct description of our experience as it is
face whitened by
power & lard

What I meant by power, I had to describe this to him when he asked
and that took up another time
the melting of the butter then it hardened again and I flicked it onto the
'Greek' pizza
just skimming

handling language
rather than a holiday from language why not just stop and say I am
stopping now and then this will be something else
our direct descriptions of face whitened by the death of

I discover within myself an eternal weakness
down there
an old blood
impairs ground,
'roseTILT'

so read don't bother writing anything except when I go down there I find
an old blood and it impairs me, eternal weakness,
nothing short of inVALID body
the skimming tactics of a reader vs the tilt of the rose

I took my petals off me

Is nothing if divorced from the spectacle of the world
this 'labial pepper'

Via Maurice Merleau-Ponty & Maggie O'Sullivan

Rungs, fences

you spent an hour with him on his rungs
you did, yes you did
and the boars tussled at the fences
and the wind could be heard where
previously it could not have been

this place was for not crying and meticulously
you have come into this space conscious
but not comprehending, at the ditch
you notice the wildlife waiting to get in

and then you made a gesture
didn't you, that was unrecorded and
unprecedented, in the field of the night
the sprinklers' tap and tap, you

could have sat down couldn't you
and when you did it was on the floor, when you
did so you called and then the emptying
and melding feeling of being named,

some old masters spoke
of the eradication of the self, the
alt- masters of an all-consuming self
but you only want one kind of master,
you only want the bio in autobiography
and the return of a familiar sound:
the ego's second falling and not landing

anyway, he was on his rungs,
and you let yourself be named anew
named through him, by another voice behind him,

there is a scalability
that's your ego on a day
when you make two mistakes
and you have been renamed

Resources from Coelbren

Some carving out, maybe,
but this can be no utopia.

Not being a strategist
I go running in the marsh,
to make something possible,
an embodied eclipse. Raymond's
possibility of resources. Bless this
freedom, a space to go piercingly
parallel with the horizon.

When the horizon is approached
it becomes footholds, an unbounded craggy place
no thin line. Past the duck pond,
the atmosphere fizzes with dread.

What is this rite for
losing you all. We humans make incisions.
In the land here it's obvious; pit-scarred to the very edge.
My feet graze its surface and the underground scars burn.

Since the beginning there was tension. And those breaks that say
you'll go on. Did my poems
once make a threshold for each lip,
that is birth that is death
between slipping, sidings, levels.

Across the way the fowl are harking.
Some ethological tracks. I can bed
into that sound and be in your quacks,
grunts and squawks. You argue over the
water that's left when the ice has encroached
but it melts soon enough.

You are not the romantic birds
the poets usually go to for kicks,
something absurd in your rough
webbed foot wading,
your rowdy quaking and waddle. Tonight
I'll be near you and you'll be sleeping, your
beaks curled into your wings. We can live together
like that in earshot for these days.

It's no utopia, I'll heat mushroom soup
from a bag in the poptyping,
then bed down in this borrowed down
of your brothers and sisters. Even the
bathroom is carpeted, love me love you.

My methodology is listening to you,
you are hope but not a resource.
Listen this little quack, little quake.
I still have a fragment of wanting to save something, sometimes,
want to, believe in something resourceful,
like if I can just think it through.

But the forces gather fast around clouds of gas
and the Canada Geese have set off into that.
They are not back yet. When the panic starts,
I could bring it back to the ducks, like breath.

The fowl appears fertile, I can't smell them from here but plan to.
I haven't counted the different species
present in the pond. They must be fucking only their brothers and sisters.

With their corkscrew parts,
their sex is wholly unfamiliar; dead-ends
the female can choose to shake unwanted fluid into,
vestigial ovaries, gang violence.

I wanted to think of them
as resource but their acts escaped me.

We're still burning in the coal they crushed people here for.

Now there are ponds for unusual mallards, birds
doing their art etc, ducks etc, sex etc. So you need not panic,
this can also be a resource.

Hunter-Actor-Poet

Poet as hunter, hyper aware of lingual networks but wearing the wrong socks and now has cold ankles. Poet as hunter totally drunk because wanted to continue a conversation with a person at a wooden table. Poet as hunter forgot to prepare for evening's poetry engagement because writing poem. Poet as hunter aware of physical needs but ignoring them in order to enter fully the mania. Hunter as poet has eyes out to every corner not wandering. No you don't have a wandering eye you have a Hunter's eye. Hunter as poet winding a dead hare around his arm. Hunter is a poet listing the names for the hare and crying because it reminds them of a lost love. Poet as hunter aware that she will need to iron her dress. Poet as hunter already selecting the green dress that does not need ironing but is the most flamboyant. Poet as hunter understanding that writing about getting ready to go outside doesn't mean actually getting ready on time. Poet as hunter really wishes she was hunter. Poet as hunter aware that writing this doesn't make them a hunter. Hunter as a real profession perhaps being too bloody, predatory, for poet. Aware also of a class of hunters he would avoid association with. Poet as hunter because hunter was their favourite word for many years. *Helwr, hela*, to find, to be the one who comes upon, *dod o hyd i*. The name of the streets she walked as a child, Hunter's mar. Huntswoman at the bar. Hunter as poet at the bar not mentioning the dead hare because she wants to be present at the wooden bar with date. Hunter aware that this is not supposed to be a date. Wants to be hunted but only in play. Hunter would like to apply make-up. Hunter aware that she has a tendency to go on and into a gathering trance. Aware of a writing trance possibly caused by the spirit of the hare they have just killed. Hunter's bar. Poet as hunter, not the same as actor as hunter but we can make some shady mingling of auras. Aura as love, evaporating off the hunter's skin, or maybe that's craft beer particles from last night. Hunter as poet is aware of the self-mythologising tendencies of poets and hates this but indulges anyway. Poet as hunter will keep their eyes open tonight, as if focused, not wandering. But if she is wearing the wrong clothes it will go wrong

Sominex love letter

I'm telling you this because of my part the mariner
and you looked such good love-triangle
across the mattress, afterwhich
I took up trade routes
vibrated in humid towers afterwhich,

weeks afterwhich, I still want to know of curls you converge
and be illumined, your curiosities
scratched on my lungs. I thought of
torches through the passage to the arena.

I want to remain ignorant of any of your gripe water,
construct enough phantasy about you, a perfect circular
present tense so I crush all reasonable behaviour
and sweat in my cotton dupatta.

I like crooner songs on a loop with a good dosage
of sominex. My issue is transience,
gliding around on the coins of the world, and I'm fair too honest.
The other lover left, taking his milkshake decision

so seriously, for twenty minutes I waited whilst
he considered the menu and I thought of you,
twice in his sleep he called me by his sister's name.

I'm telling you this because his mainly open eye wasn't enough
and the secret availability of me is hopeful
for at least a season in you. I've got collections of swimming pool pics
to show you and it's better you come to

me all at once in a truck crash but,
well, movement in the spine should be treasured, and I'm
tomorrow to set out for another pavilion
where I'll recall phantasy-frags not fully formed

just peaking and troughing as I pace a mat then
writ a message to you as I fall asleep on the keys
at the names, my breath tonight
dispatching myself on drowsy meds and Madras filter coffee.

Yesternight I had such banal dreams,
but there were sounds of what creature was it, simian, feline.
I know I have lucki sandals and you're in winter.
The ultimate ribbon market for goblin things is between here and home,

and Christina Rossetti gazing hands face eyes up, not touching the page, the poem.
Now to write you have to stare at a screen for
stratified curls to come full in French twist. Touch the poem,

the letters. I know the truck crash was my least happy trope.
I like to stick to the old metaphor grid
not go off piste from the format, for you, take it seriously.
When I called you were writing songs

in your second language. I'm a serious poet,
won't provide alliteration for insta captions.
I burn vigils in the shrine of Christina's
century, losing petals to Jesus and Krishna.

Sands exist in the future, doing rugged.
This is my refrigerated grid or love poem chewed in the third stomach
so it came out uncrisp but crimped
still pink, under my fourth hemisphere touch.

The kind of cranberry stain on a table cloth, a flush the
Bosporus does and raki stippled light like that,
or the time I swam in a modernist swimming pool
and emerged hypothermic, I dedicate this to you.

Though I only met you five years later when vibrating
in the kebab shop. Often I wonder
if I'm only attracted to other narcissists,
and now, having started this aimlessness venturing as

seamen, this flat earth, the fact that semen floats, the fact of monkey urine.
I forgave the baby monkeys because of their,
well, you know, do I have to say it, cuteness,
not sure what this has to do with you

but your hair is so nice, that's all, and enough
I need someone to make intellectual milkshake decisions,
not in five years' time, just a bit rugged
like the men in Amrita's bonk book set in Rajasthan

Sandstorm, 1991, it didn't make her enough
money to buy a fridge, or write serious books, but like her I take romance
serious, I want to be a love poet
seamen on the edges converging to you hope so

Carotid properties

weepsweep our carotid line   running between head and forest
the cervical spine where they puul
fraem-a   left-headed genital seep   or is it   sweep

      sweepland   left the floor a strewnnstew   sck   prss
heavens homs homage to her   polypus driving this neck   this
neck pulled up puppet

i-love

the swoonshirt the   admirable holler of wet window

                                              to the forests

and so nothing except to learn and   learn out of the lean
scratch

the fraz-hurt Novembers   scud-*gravelled*   *his philology*
scared-of-crow   burst

how do you smile any more   anyhow so jilted
                  a hom-age of hers / 'its crimson centre' / Houma

carrying carotid between the spreading out from head to forest the main vein runs

you're worried at the mesh

the net of running threads red threads between neck and skull

two carotid veins
a dualism – union
working in humming   eye pro-ducted pro=duced produced an I and
re-prod   duct tape around its edges

one her-november to another heart-nosed, cross-thicket outward and
the carrying causeway

causeway to circle of willis and *to the forests*

but was that plantation or forest   ?   pur-gluck
find the subclavian or the innominate arteries

and the causeway arterial bond

the space between heaving cave-brain and the forests

make a hom to homs and the homelie   lean out of the latch

feet touch down on the causeway   be deliberate as icicle drea
cross sections of 0Sul   kra   crane candid the bird hide

where his   yew   his   cervical too
        learn from her homa soma houma   nov-embers

a limb brust a bust a clavian bow   must we   e-e-e
stripped scand0 scandalice scale0sul sulsi

*

NOTE: In David Jones's *Anathemata* I find Thomas Willis of 'the
Circle of Willis'. This circle is the destination in the brain of the
blood that flows through the carotid arteries.

   Thomas Willis (1621–1675), one of the Oxford Experimentalists, a
royalist, a friend of Locke, a physician in the marketplace in Abingdon.
Willis was on close terms with Susan Holder (1627–1688), sister of
Christopher Wren and wife of William Holder. And Susan Holder,
'rare she-surgeon', was skilled in the art of healing wounds

   'It ought not to be forgott the great and exemplary love
   between this Doctor and his vertuose wife, who is not lesse
   to be admired, in her sex and station, then her brother Sir
   Christopher; and (which is rare to be found in a woman) her
   excellences doe not inflate her. Amongst many other guifts
   she haz a strange sagacity as to curing of wounds, which she

39

does not doe so much by presedents and reciept bookes, as by her owne excogitancy, considering the causes, effects, and circumstances. His majestie king Charles II, 167-, had hurt his...hand, which he intrusted his chirurgians to make well; but they ordered him so that they made it much worse, so that it swoll, and pained him up to his shoulder; and pained him so extremely that he could not sleep, and began to be feaverish...told the king what a rare shee-surgeon he had in his house; she was presently sent for at eleven clock at night. She presently made ready a pultisse, and applyed it, and gave his majestie sudden ease, and he slept well; next day she dressed him, and in...perfectly cured him, to the great griefe of all the surgeons, who envy and hate her.'

Fairy Business

Just a light weight pinecone (rest, get some rest now),
little little teeth, but very sharp
they eat the shapelets and the poems.

In the night these fairies jumbled
up my sock pairs and now
a light shines through the holiest ones,

a cheap joke for my fairy lord who came in
on CAM4 to ask for the socks with holes in, specifically.
I think nothing of this fetish,
myself thought often of fairy conditions
where everything milken lit becomes sensation
palpating undergarment drawers—! Golden thimbles of ale—!

It's a personal thing
or cash cash get the bill, or actually
they dealt in tiny loaves, or actually
they came round rarely via the backlane gwli,
but exceptions to the rule make the rule.

I sometimes find my lover's laughter creepy
so I speak to my fairy lord who never irks,
but conditions in the forest become too alkaline,
lichen falters, mulch is heavily metalled
a dairy farm across the way keeps strip lights on all night
pumping pump pump the milken light—!

The pinecone's magical properties are something to do with the
gland above the penis or pineal or pituitary gland
it doesn't matter it's all third eye pressing through

But nowadays I need specificity. I already lost one friend
to gaia.com and I need some new

vocabulary to get her back so
I take a map of the local bomb craters
a walk that will collapse me weight me
make a walk that will sink me into bramble pits into history future,

but I need quality overtrousers for the rolling,
for the suckering tripwires
the brambles pull you back pull me back
to the wood and the mosses over every horizon.

My fairy lord laughed once
and that was enough (I must've told a good joke once, that was enough)
at least enough for a poem to be squeezed out
and a small cup of airy ale from blackberries, (think what that would taste of) yes
fairy conditions are the conditions
of passage, the yet–not,
conditions in the gwli, in the llyn. T.T. does not
stand for twee tat. Sometimes
their conditions went on in the back palaces
of egos and when I came back everything was upsidedown

I didn't want to blame my poor friend
so I made a porridge out of pine nuts,
the butter rose to the top & was rich enough,
I am not a prince presenting himself to the
fairy motorcade, bartering for pinenuts,
charcoal nodes. I am just here in
the gwli waiting for their havoc

To the east

To the east, walk across that space you can see
The meadow is an apex of what was perfect
In the trees beyond, you find someone's shelter
This is the intended walk, it finds the sites by itself
Pollinators visit the spot where yesterday two of you
A polity here, the string between the nownesses
It wasn't a smart move to swing so freshly towards this
Admire his sunburn turned to rud this is the colour
Of demigods but it rocks away from a summer like
Objectivity. To the east I saw my own path

Blod rite

Blod's meta   morphosis

Feathers in shreds
Or so the story goes + out into the night flies eye in the dark
                                        hands of feathers five
Foretaste tasted like petals

A lover falls into the join in my inter
Lover + green rush
Your bounteous watch
Ancestress woven from ditch

Chrysalis   pairs
of eyes in the wood
    be in my spine + over my face
Flutter (m)orph sin flush
flutes for crone

The untold part flitters a
crown of meadowsweet
bracelet of derwen
anklet of birch
the catkins are in here too

      Orpheus was Pets at Home
      Pentheus was gruel
      Euripides farts long and guttural

Careful, nothing is foreclosed yet

Says a chalice, says amber
Says I-am, the implement,
Says spine, out of pine
Says ever rose, says scream fetch,

or fetish. Says the pale of water,
says Lech. Says grandiose,
says home wood
Says algae, says grape perk

rock. So we can set to work in beauteous rage
& can rebirth, in ash flower,
can fall into lipbalm and shrinelike.

Lover nuanced on me flush with her cardio
She was willing to be secret unsaid

dip thrice + pumpwaith
Mer me   over   crane
             Cross   immerse/emerge immer emer mer mer

Affectual, sandaless, soft oak
It was good to meet her he said

Parakeet aloft my green visitor
or any everyday bounty

There's an Isle off the shining foreshore
& the moon of Porthcawl

I never no, vanilla, no
lillicking whispered
true nocturnal off balance

Each limb wrote you I
I was made for loving you
But I loved another in the wood
so you meta'd me, babe, mead-wort

and bolognaise denial,
a ring of precious rave gods
Jarvis, Fritoj, Julian and Lisa

Now I need an ash tree aureole
Or cennau circle

Cen the imperfect medium for Jack
Alice the imperfect medium for Alan
Cen the rib on the oak, a patina
Half algae half moss

Cen in the medium of Hadewijch
Cen saint of lichen and of hedge
saint of the patch of ditch

So I am (re)born of the lichenate

& my floristry is flying to you by night
foretelling of death, but whose?
May it be the best and hoped for

Etc, green freedom, etc, altarwise by owl-bite
fforest-library saflax brow
meadowheight

Wassail

My old grey mare, blood-lead my LED eye.
My new libation, like a novel.

Then revival tremors in the down light:
making it up in the soft play hard den.

I knew the words but not the tune:
the wind at the door every morning.

Severed grin, technology for snapping;
how came the blood on your history?

Creatures who unchoke the bridle
they are cake crusher and jigging

folkloric mirror / folkloric muse.

*

When Mari appeared, the woman in the bakery froze and so did I.
My companion noted we seemed 'away with fairies'. Some things
just give you that feeling, maybe that's their folkloric wish. You
didn't feed the fairies enough cider, you told your nephew they
have sharp teeth etc etc. Revival rites can give bad Teutonic
feelings; insignias on lapels, blood bonding, mummers who vote
Tory, etc etc. You avert your eyes away, think fair folk. Any
meaning in Mari's streamers you have to make up and yet the
lore folds into this, your new years.

for Roddy Lumsden

Fear and the Piano

The repeated key
      a haptic stored over sedimental time // *I*-work

    Or work within fear's crease   where the breathing organs swell and
    contract
    In the membrane between me and world

Piano lessons
Piano practice
Piano play

Ten seconds and an answer's coming

There is this instant   you've allowed   herenow   for a later and a before
or a flipped now

The perceptual order has given you an instant
The piano also has its instant
The shapes I found + soundlightcolourmemoir are combined into a sense
that flickers

So what membrane fixed and unfixed   once and rolled over   and then
the yet to be

The implications of such a flicker
The implications of such piano

    Fear taking time out   obligatio-membranes bordered with fear

Overwhelm   :   well that's so broad

Take instructions from the piano
Fold into instruct   extruct   instructions from the young   from the learner,
                             Or from the other learners
                             try

Piano and kidney	kidney communicates	*what are these and why*
Sedimented body	geologic kidney	fear explains or does it exceed
Mnemonic body	Mnemonic movement	Mnemonia
Pam / pam lei	parallels	staves
ancestorial fears	the animal instant	the courage to

Striatum

Crested, wool wet, all in a mode
of raging love. Warring with the
fabric of connection. The dangerous light
might not yet reach the inner flesh, but you have tried.

When the police raided bookshops,
it wasn't so long ago either,
when tattoos & holes newly filled in.
Damp towels. Cleansing daily the grit off,

coffee rites, florality, these are recent. Could it be guilt
or shame, maybe it's both. Could it be responsibility
or complicity, maybe it's both. Could it be depression
or anxiety, maybe it's both. My media is body.

So is yours. I'm troubled, you said. So tear my
poem out of its carapace. Subsist on
it, I don't care. The romance of the rose takes up the
daytime and the sleep of colour can be peony.

The romance of placing things
in their correct zone. So at the opportune time
you can come back to them. Dry towels, coffee, poetry,
flowers and sleep its carapace.

But in minor fevers, nights collect the slight times
when they judged you. Think instead of bookshop romance
where I miss you wholeheartedly. Or cleansing
in dangerous light. A volume

on a city unvisited. There is an incremental killer
in your swig. Veins drain of peony.
Things drop through the body medium
like salts should and nutrients. The trace

of someone's ankle tag. Some real gathering
is desired. *Votive* is linked to *desire* at branch and root.
I will ask you later if you approve.
How will I judge your answer in the bookshop

of nodes and clean towels. A swig
takes place over and over in the striatum. Stitchy
little poem strands work the fascia
and should not be exposed to dangerous light.
Poetry's utility as peony as rage.

Rig Works (Wonder / Damage)

1 *Oil rig gift shop*

My word is enough, is it not?
Daddy loves you, is it not?

The gifts are listed : records sham rough
teddy in overalls, early trolls,
Take it up with a
Another Father Figure
Please

Two weeks on two weeks off
on shore off
off shore on
this ingrained pattern
but it didn't hurt
did it
it's ok

I'm ok   OK   I'm happy for my lilac clothes

Aberdeen psilocybin
moving through the stealth of
Friday night
A pattern so tight that each anticipation hurts

The daddies pick up super tangle free brushes from the in-flight shop
And I decide to buy dad a coffee grinder

oil rig exotic / rough neck occidental
Log jam ethic / yeh so it is / mud logger

Two week friction put my hand against
enough
is it enough

On the super-sickness of the open, I wanted to go home to the steel islands.
Petro-geo-sifter, adrift
                   on North's flexion,
                       its compass,
                       its treeless decks,
Ocean Nomad umbilicised to the wells until derrickhands unleash her on
buoyant ribs.
         Ocean Nomad
         assembled Trosvik Framnaes, 1975, ghost-yard
         of oil-boilers,
         steel riggers,
berth place of *Endurance* and other Antarctic scoopers; of killers
     – the *Jason*,
     the *Pelican*,
     the *Frey*,
     those looking for other ocean nomads.
Ocean Largess.

Ocean Nomad still drilling Kells, Staffa field, with three mud pumps.
Ocean Nomad,
     semisub driller
     and distributor of long-wearing embroidered crew tees –
         daggy red,
         frayed collar,
         pelagic sun bleach.
                   Ocean Nomad. Sitting
twelve hours with a tray of sandy sludge. Smells unlight, his long awake arms.
Musk of   helicopter,
                 taxi, jet.
         A t-shirt, twelve years of ambergris. Twelve days bound for home
to home's tepid bath,
                home's awakened mess.

Think of a diamond body
the diamond body is a light body and the rainbow body a multiple body the
most sacred body the subtle body the blod-body of bliss
I can tell you how it affects

I work/fold your fascination into this diamond   its hard edges are useful
I can learn how to cradle the diamond body   this spacious cut surface

    When I was a child I had a book that explained the oil rig. My
    parents must've felt I needed this book because the oil rig was
    where my father spent half of his time. In the book was a diagram
    of the drill. The drill had spirals of diamonds corkscrewed around a
    cone. Resisting a phallic interpretation here, I wish to focus on the
    parts of the drill bit. The pictures showed the diamonds had been
    cut in order to cut. The diamond is selected to drill the ocean floor
    because it is the hardest substance in the world. The diamond is
    not just adornment it is the hardest extractor. It is a mineral to find
    the other minerals to burn up and change our mineral air forever.

A crumple in this, her nails

    toxicity report: grapple   breath was only   surfaces

Licks the inner intimate, ex-timate   when I invoke I swell

Middle Sea's ripple   and that's the life for me   Meer Sea's
slight juncture   this way that way   I swell

Functioning   I heard ovary   when you said   [   ]

Middle seams open water   Off land Off shore by islands in the oil
tension so much palmarosa   all of it functioning except where it Off
or Offers itself   its sole self   burnt helix   bream   diamond drill

In a lightly flecked rose   save for a solvent   and a mild aberration

Lacey

Lace loops all over our gestures, women crocheting with their
thumbs little loop work   rep and rep rep rep   into one hole
at a time spreads into the greatest floral spreading ever

Other women looped into my words gave me a napkin for the
blackberry stain, made notes on my hand movements, gestures,
wrote me a note that read: take the tram to the lace market

I linked the texts   I mean textures   together for incorporation
cats cradle rite   I bring these talks to fold into the veld of the
lace layer cake   make a mix

Isla Negra wove a lace collab, Karü Mapu Tierra Negra
Inspired this new needle swerve, a piece for the stain rumpled
porridge sustenance   these island papas sustain   Pampas
comes crinoline or lidded   all the solidarities folded rep and into
and swallow rep

A continuous knit or was it lace or was it weave or spin into the
little spaces between the yarn knots.   in those gaps.   mouths
singing aquamarine

Tik the tact think constraints like a need to gossip over tweed
bashing or the fact that winter night starts at 3pm.   or a loop
loop loop and pay for my babe's basket

Skin pocks crater shallow hole basin dip, imagine if that was land
if that scale caressed the sharing caressed the limey pearls hands
hard or soft or picked

Line in the lace or weave tick   don't stop or move over   from
the floor to the arms this movement is also a weave a women's
flick or a flip splay the arc of a rep rep

'The body may remain erotic, sexual, desired, desiring, and yet
still be votive – marked and written over in a text of stroke
and gesture discovered by my creative female will.'
CAROLEE SCHNEEMANN

This would be a retrospective

This would be a retrospective
in the conditional

I learnt my minoritised language.

This was after the new error
In the error before the era, a lost wax fish
of animated brass and ruby.

This would be a time I had to disentangle
from the personal crises of my employers,
and the demand to declare all allegiance at all times,
from a confusion of me and you.

I found a pink marker and made swipes at the whiteness, learnt elemental words.
Stayed ether
I did not know where to place my political direction so it seeped into all.
I had desire for bright and deep, could they co-exist, stay ether

I made notes for transmitting through multiple spaces
but such a movement had to be dis-imperial.

I wrote 'awgrymu' & 'gaethon nhw...ysbeil' in my notes
now I'm llongddrylliad.
Stay *ether*, everything made in the mouth, can be combined.

This was a year I stood between many people and sweated,
I wanted social and shared, I wanted to give over.
We both made transfers of equity.

Medha was reading the classics.
I heard the sound of Gauri Lankesh's name repeated

I made a brainstorm on the word *freedom*,
for a festival of freedom I was Britishly attending
whilst trying to become less British. I asked after
the nature of freedom.
All of this lead to a discomfort on stage at Freedom Food Festival.
And an act of valiance on Mamta's part
to obtain food ahead of schedule.

Savita said, write feminist poems.
One morning I was observed sketching a Royal Enfield;
I was trying to recall that rhyme about leaping.
Contexts implode in the notebooks chronically,
so that shots in the back sit beside recipes
for chickpea salad. What about kites?
What about coloured markers? Surveillance?
Big paper for body shapes?

We became sculptural for forty minutes.
We produced reams and chanted.
From the swing the students sang. Small leaf bowls were needed.

I was travelling or was I dissipating towards a body votive.
I would make myself vow; I would vow to give my body
but to whom and what or how

the earth, magnified, a sinking would be required.
A burial? I thought I detected a hard smell of molecules
which included worms.

This was also the time I toppled over and over
pivoting from the toes. De-imperialising,
de-oblivioning, de-entitling a body. In hope.

If it could be emptied which it could not
If it could be offered which it could not
If it could be joined which it could
Might it reconfigure
Might it disalign?

I wrote the words *adfeilion babel*
and the first few ruins were everything.
Another tower toppled.

Gauri Lankesh, Gauri Lankesh.
We moved by more portents towards the worst frameworks.
Increasingly a curdling grip on the bodies

grinds further. And then something.
She held my feet in her lap
and I wondered how she found
rhizomes through the soles.

If I could uncouple my gestures from those of
the Company and its inheritors.
If I could breath alongside everyone.
If I could expand horizontally and stay ambiguous
stay amorous, stay able to taste delicious. Stay ether.
Amrita spoke of an unfolding.

I made steps around the building,
so I still dream of an architectural mandala.
Moving around and towards multiple centres
convergent, through petalled rooms,
lotus hearths. Stretched out in the L shaped room,
badam leafed, we heard the vegetable vendors calling.

In this time, searching for a political method,
that is a body votive, a body social.
Repeating a vow, saying all kinds of words
to activate social muscles, en-act I said

and we are still unfolding. Yes
I had a moral kernel and it wanted to emerge.
Liminality is not an end in itself, we desire the threshold
which unfolds towards other thresholds.

Look at the tourists in the city looking up
they are pretending they are alone,
I too am one of them, wandering agog under the architecture,
very together, trying to be present awfully.
Through the filter of visions, I stood between the people
in the dreams of other people dreaming and sweated

I made acts and theorisations, in the conditional,
I made acts
Dwi'n dysgu fy iaith leiafrifol

Tír na nÓg again

Youth & young thingness,
as yearlings, in animated talking
we have no thought of the other issue,
no thought of the other nows
no place like this home on the tennis court
no heaviness over whether to have a cigarette
pieces of a place I once ventured, it was called the rufts
it was a soup of lust-envy-greed etc
it was chips the texture of fudge
an inability to wear clothes that fit
oil surfacing on the skin hourly so I used a special blotting paper
bodyspraying, ways of keeping the discharges in, dabbing
jabbing at the youngness, fried pizza,
fried double cheese, fried pudding with friend,
oh I have to eat this forever this lonely screwball icecream
with a bubble gum at the bottom
another home another dreaming I was from another culture
dreaming I had better shoes
stuck wanting a new chapter on the sticky gym apparatus
what if I could never leave the mud shin pads
and never leave the playing field,
lungs burning through weather,
could go round the corner, the corridor
forever on a loop, could stratify out through the glitch
a school architecture that kept us moving
circular that was squared,
an art deco grid that haunts fairly regular
when we ran around like that in the loop

Wear the anklet as a mask

A poetics

1 *Separation: conditions of the poem*

This ritual begins with strange literature festival. Roald Dahl is brought back to life and the audience faints; a line of sweet dancing girls makes us cry. A TV screen is wheeled in. It resembles the machines we would watch at school in the AV room. Its screen bears the black and white close up of a tongue sticking out. Closer and closer we move into the image of the tongue on the screen. We are beamed into the canyons of the tongue.

After waking from this dream at my parents' house, I find the anklet my mother acquired in India in the 1970s. I would play with this belled anklet in these rooms when I was a child. Today it recalls the grey tongue in the dream screen.

It makes a good costume to wear over the mouth.

As I handle this object the experiment forms: writing in costume / semi-mask. The proposal the dream offers is to wear this anklet as a mask and improvise / write.

As usual I begin with collage and run through a bodily warming, the repetition of words and actions. The time brackets are tight: three minutes on, three minutes off. Even so, endurance is at play, Tim Etchells' words 'going too far' are in my mind.

The movement I make is a gasp in, a whole tensing intake of breath an 'oh' with the lips closing around the sound to make it 'ahm.' Or is it an 'oam' or 'aum'? Hands tense, the shoulders curve in on each. Upon repetition, I find the need to breathe out: a rhythm of four big swallows and a big out breath. The top half of my body rhythmically tenses in the sound, the bathroom fan is humming and it resonates with the sound emerging out of me. The in, the in, the in. I start feeling faint and wobbly, a head blood rush speed up the wobble the high or is it lack or too much oxygen.

What exactly is hyperventilating? Now might not be the moment to ask, but it is only three minutes... I cannot wait for it to be over, a little movement or action a pause. I try one breath in one big out. Three minutes expand like never before. Finally, the alarm goes; I must give myself 3 minutes rest on the floor. Here my internal voice returns, I think of recent conversations I have had about rest. That urge: one cannot just lie here, resting is hard. Earlier today I wondered if the thing I'm calling ritual poetry is just giving oneself a rest? A pause from the desperate rush for production...

*

The Oam is a signal we swallow. It is a raft of air, that is an internal burst of oxygen. It is creaturely and it pours out of us on a fourth iteration. Back out the shoulders push it. It is a mini spirit, an inspiration, a spiri inspired. Then it must be expired and as it is, it passes into us as an irrigation of oxygen.

What if each bodily function were a deity or a goblin or a creature and this formed a round ball like the Borg of *Peer Gynt*, or in this case the creature of hot dry carpet air coming into my lung frame. I am a frame for this ball of inspiration,

> yr awelon o awen (heh)
>
> Granular muses in and out.

Transpiration – moving across a point towards syncope.

Opening out between breaths? I think about collapsing and dying which is what I felt in the trance in that seminar room in East London in the Eurydice jam.

*

Now for the swallow with the costume tongue on. Downstairs my parents are preparing food. I am fortunate to have their vessel for this strange fear.

3 minutes in and laughing at the image of myself in the mirror. The anklet worn over the mouth looks like fetish wear. The ritual of dressing up – putting on and off restraints or adornment. The liminality of carnival, a subspace.

But there is another side to this object on my face. This anklet/mask also recalls bondage in its violent sense: mouth pieces, tongue bits and enslavement. Women in bondage as signalled by the anklet, in some parts and times. Now it is in my mouth and I breath. Three in, one out again hard. I don't feel faint this time.

But then a 'thing' happens when I lie down to rest. Gravity sucks the chain into my mouth and I am holding it in my teeth.

My father calls me to say food is ready and I call back something with no contours. I worry about tetanus, poisoning, from the metal, an allergic reaction on the inside of my mouth. And I think about those forced to wear metal. Then my teeth start to chatter and the metal crunches. The movement of the jaw happens without my choosing, beginning to tremble without control.

In the slimmest of time intervals, I have had reminder of a violence. We play at something dark sometimes, a dark game that is resemblance. Play is not the real of enforcement, it is just a brief embodiment. This is the work of the actor. But this 'going too far' allows a wild surge as the body lurches.

Even so, I am still lucid so I get up and go to the mirror, my chain mouth still chattering. My parents are calling me again. The mirror image of my face. I film it. It looks terrible; the chain pulls over my top lip.

Only twenty minutes has passed. Tea is pea and ham and parsley sauce and potatoes from the allotment. This is a very good threshold meal.

From the jumble of metal against teeth, words of any kind,

One pressed out the bone limits by bile // who was it a culpability, a winning, a young invertebrate, a helmet that is a shell

I wondered about here in this liminal, on those upper limits of atomic patter, some hedge-topia of poetics, some haven?

                                 And down here in dys-used-topia

    a hogen/merch/bodan/eneth/roces was standing on the pasture or was it coke, a coke pile before the war or was it after the big bang.

Matter was always locked and fixed ready to burn; it falls apart to atoms and quarks, that is to say there are waves propelling. I find one of the pieces of the past in this narrative, fragmented.

Peopled with ghosts this smoking world, their shoes unfixed to the floor. They come closer and a crowd gathers gently chanting in a murmur that jumped from one shore to another, from one mouth to another, a chant from another transition. The elderly enslaved people, Trinidad 1834, at the point of 'abolition' and on being told they must do another six years of 'apprenticeship' they began chanting, 'Pas de *six ans*. Point de *six ans*'

                     *

Atom   who is this baroque language of human

                         a girl on a coke pile in Fochriw
atom and atom focused   some freedom to play

  one of the atoms came by them, was a piece from a bigger piece dismantled sequentially // one wanted –

            to be reassembled, re- assembled, re-sembled

                     *

A mask perhaps of chain, perhaps a sheet of fine chain placed over the mouth, but not restricting only obscuring speech, somehow alluring oneself, somehow tonguing oneself; restraint when consented not to speak until, and then this consent may be given to restrict us in freedom, then this gesture is a gesture of force not the force of force, but the force of resembling other forces, so you can hear the elders chanting: not six years, over six years, and then this year

atoms knit then fall away, asking when does a metaphor become its subject? What is the threshold between playing bondage and bondage? What is play and when is it not? When is it going too far?

Wear the anklet as a mask

To speak through the chain veil
to speak through the mesh
to speak through the anklet
to speak through the manacle
to speak through the headdress
to speak through the bit
to speak through the limit
to speak through the tang
to speak through clusters of crunch, a little zinc or magnesium
to speak through a metaphorical manacle that gestures remind us of
to speak through fortune if that is to know what I have not known
to speak through the fortune of play, to play with the not knowing
to speak through this jiggling movement of the teeth on the baubles of
metal and realise a fear to speak through and write
to not write of it as something more or less than it was
to not write at all
to move in sympathy and speak through sympathy
to speak or write through only one position that is not to speak for others
to listen whilst speaking in the costume
to find out who is speaking
to see the vision of self in mirror reminded one of an other
to work with that mirror other

       so then what is costume then?
    is costume metonymy or metaphor?

  how to even consider playing another person?

      suppose the costume allows the playing in the subspacetime

      suppose the mask is more than costume

      what is costume and playing and 'going too far' ?

        what is costly in costume?

what headache does the costume produce and what does it cost?

can the costume itself speak and does it cost to speak?

does it costumise me to consider the other wearers of the mask I have metonymically mimicked by accident?

suppose the mouth sounds so terrible to itself it started to feel so terrible, so that I longed for peas and ham and a good chest of hair to lean on

suppose there is one who is locked in a spacetime of sub, and has consented to be left there

suppose there is another one who is locked in a spacetime of dark and has not consented to be left there

is it metaphor or metonymy that links them?

the costume also depends on where one is standing, is it inside or outside?

moving into the tongue in the film was different to moving into the tongue metaphor

an object could be a metonymy for enslavement and for playtime

I suppose the discomfort of that contrast

consider the comfort of the contrast of peas & ham & parsley sauce vs the discomfort of what was glimpsed in the costume

the costume left bits in my face, in my mouth

the discomfort of the chain on the top lip, a threshold

the chattering of the mask

the brief taste of metal, brief tang of an other pain

Hafod Jam: Documentation

In the moment you're reading you look real
how to
        look real when you're [bookish]

A high kick
side glance

What did the body learn from this lengthy panting   painting
in
        Is it oh lord of the caves   *is it*
Awareness is not easy   is it

Rolling each string towards this one
to pull on this one to pull in   a wheel inside a wheel

A   side project is a score for
Me when I am real
                Or is it wilderness

So to pause, ask which mark is the right mark, ask what is the physical
manifestation of the cosmic problem?

Here are some bad vibes the body moves through: Vodafone stole my
family love / such care taken over the Vivian's dog graveyard at Clyne /
Fascist tyrants repeatedly elected / Half the students in this school were
absent due to Scarlet fever, says the notes for winter 1865 / dullened
poisoned soil / Hapticality's Hope(less)hope

What happened when copper emerged in the hall
when it emerged as strong history?   Clue: it's not ghostly

Note the transferences to the dead and their ochre   their colour palette

When you crawl towards the camera, something is *interesting*, but then it's
gone

Oxidised water seeped out of the old mine   dead orange   re-gen

Regeneration was the joke of the post-industrial,
the whole 1990s a warehouse of plastic

When you pulled your arms apart, for example, as if drawing a bow
the space that opens up
this join is the [   ]
My cursive best

The gaze of the world
The gaxe of the world
The gas of the world
The grave of the world
The gain of the world
                    Is the camera lens a threshold through which the
world stops (or starts) to see you? Let this threshold of previous cycles
melt and feel the world as some other doorway

Could they all link up if you just pulled the string? if you wind in the
whole length of the string, will you regain everything you have lost?

Breathing and breathing the link unsevered
Snipping and snipping the fates at the string

Will not die till the beast is killed   time's up   a breath a block
Between memorising the words and remembering and forgetting and
remembering and forgetting
Repeating until   the gap between recalled restored word   and

Tuning or layering or linking in the knot to act out
                    Now alone in the Victorian school, the rain coming in the
          broken window;
          a circle where the camera's gaze can fall
                    Are ritual and documentation mutually exclusive?

Awareness is not easy is it oh Alama Prabhu, oh AK Ramanujan, oh Lord of the Caves, oh translator!

Claustrophobia, which is what we're in   hunt   hela   the
site for history   a lot of   I DON'T KNOW
Datrys / drysfa

That opening   the jar   *i get trouble even opening a honey jar*   stalled
the body made me REAL

What moving says

The sun that you were born in and die under
a maw of something   it could be a great   overturn   so we move
  into the place   none of us have ever seen anything of. Harbingers?
you said.

Listening hard in jazz dirges   and to songs for those thrown overboard
in mangroves   in plague tales   told by the one sheltering candle
grim 'we'   and born   so we go   hands out
towards recognition towards something there   that takes indiscriminately
& eventually claims all   it sees them coming and by their voices,
feels taken, almost reborn   vaporous even   at night the voices
their predictions and predilections

and someone hammering away at a   hammer
In the skimming lightwork, you think you'll own this but you want help
NEED IT
Yes, the lips hurt   who am I to address you directly   ur spinal column
ur teeth

there is the death of pollinators to consider around here
you surge in a bag and bring the results to me   flea size hurting, sorcerer
ache gladly   or ungladly the meaning's come in the room, tired   wants soup
makes a strange surge now   some halfmoon 'intention' which is actually money

they're giving bad cosmo-logic advice out there on the waves
but this dance makes the opposite
because there are so few fish left   a sonnet   a knot of you in a wide web

this dance being once a fear poem   that turned on its darkest hour
now it hopes it is hope against   and all that other dust   a whole life
a whimsy me inside,   from some barely tangible core muscle   towards a
great phantom

a wise crack in that second   then out of this and   oh am I not changed
　　　am I?   am I not chastened   if not changed?

in time to stop   and now by organ light and the world of new 'souls'
　　　by the world of takers and here, some givers
someone lets you go home to the world

Llewaidd, Chauvet/Uplands

Passageway, night time. Us
that's all of us, originated here,
humblised, born under makeshift
parti-frames in brief festivals.

The telling of a spell is now downvoted
lines are ground into the light
coming as we do from conflict
also the rift, that's all of us,
mind blank, shoulders hunched
a domino effect to divinatory cards,
the blush of four callow men
and one woman somewhere out there

is it enough to come from just after Babel
yn wreiddiol so there's no need
for cheap purple cloth or fortune bots
it's enough to come from Chauvet
or Lascaux or in between; enough to be original just once
sleeping in till 11.40, your lover
has a scratch on their face from last night
and we also came from that violence
too, of tavern hulks, coked up long-arms,
haven destroyers. Half of us then crawl along the floor

through the wooden corridor to the toilet to spit blood
the half who have to kick and flail,
remember we half are road-body under the law;
this dys-carriage kicks us into not-life
under the name of life, the vessels that we are
though the vessels of us can be obscured, layered
under swathes of pretty dresses and symbology.

But gestation sprawls beneath the gauze,
a cubist lottery; saying hi to a life-death world
you quickly scrawl poems in your new-old languages
heb chwedlau anghredadwy, heb wely gwaedlyd
os welwch chi'n dda yn y wawr newydd
Llewesau yn Chauvet,
is it enough to come from lionhood
where beasts rub genderless against each other

we are not lionised yet, making up lives
in ochred blood, step back
stand up to see ourselves llewaidd
the two lovers still nuzzling on the cave wall
overhead, briefly we can be born backwards
head foretelling the portal
stepping back into the light llewbennog

Mother of OYSTER

a vehicle one foot
a vehicle an other foot
a vehicle one hand, bivalvic
a vehicle: manual contact

the clam stretch
I got you in a market in which country
City of Flea
equinoxic

the opposite of en pointe
is grounded, is one thing, is buried
no telos in here
heightened in the dark room
ar cyhydnos

NOTES & ACKNOWLEDGEMENTS

'Mieri' recalls work by Stuart Cooke and Paulo Huirimilla Oyarzo with the Humedal Antiñir in Puerto Montt, Chile (2019); Simon Whitehouse's *Walking between Craters* (2010) in Swansea/Abertawe; Cofiwch Dryweryn and Menna Elfyn's *Mwyara* (1976).

'Dick Joke Poem' refers to *Safe* directed by Todd Haynes (1995) with Julianne Moore.

'I Have Taken Many Forms Before I Took This One' refers to Cad Goddeu from the *Book of Taliesin*.

'Scores for ritual poetry' includes reference to David Jones's *Anathemata* (1952) and *Adfeilion Babel: Agweddau Ar Syniadaeth Ieithyddol Y Ddeunawfed Ganrif* by Caryl Glyn Davies (UWP, 2000).

'Phenomenology of cut up' is made after Maggie O'Sullivan and Maurice Merleau-Ponty.

'Resources from Coelbren' refers to Raymond Williams.

'Carotid Properties' references Maggie O'Sullivan's poems and David Jones' *Anathemata* (1952). The found text on Susan Holder is from John Aubrey's *Brief Lives* (1693) from the entry on William Holder.

'Fear and the Piano' replies to Scott Thurston's poem (2019).

'Striatum' is after Derek Jarman's *Chroma* (1995).

'Lacey' refers to Karü Mapu Tierra Negra collective in Chile (2018). With thanks to Lila Matsumoto and Renee Gladman for the napkin.

'Wear the anklet' refers to Tim Etchells and Forced Entertainment's *Certain Fragments* (1999), *Peer Gynt* by Henrik Ibsen (1867) and an animation made on the Borg by Kristian Pederson (2016), to *Tír na nÓg* by T. Gwynn Jones (1909).

'Hafod Jam' is made after Allama Prabhu in translation by A.K.

Ramanujan in *Speaking of Shiva* (1973) and Fred Moten and Stefano Harney's *The Undercommons* (2013). With thanks to Hafod Community Centre.

Much of the poetry in this collection emerged from doctoral research into ritual, performance and embodied practice (*Threshold Moves: A Ritual Poetry Practice*, 2021, University of Salford). I offer my deepest gratitude those who helped realise this work, especially to Scott Thurston and Kate Adams. Also thanks to: Kimberly Campanello, Katie Jones, Síofra McSherry, Amy McCauley, Ghazal Mosadeq, Taraneh Mosadegh, Carlos Sotto Roman, Joey Frances, Nat Raha, Camilla Nelson, Nathan Walker, Renee Gladman, Lila Matsumoto, Maggie O'Sullivan, Rhys Trimble, Peter Jaeger, Tim Atkins, Jeff Hilson, Richard Parker, Jessica Pujol Duran, Geraldine Monk, Steven Hitchins, Zöe Skoulding, Lily Robert-Foley, Wanda O'Connor, Mamta Sagar, Savita Singh, Medha Singh, Amrita Shah, Kieron Smith, Ashok Vish, Beth Greenhalgh, Penny Hallas, Lyndon Davies, Tess Wood and Taz Rahman.

Thanks to the editors following publications for publishing versions of some of these poems: *Geopoetics* (2021), *No Matter* (2019), *Spells* (Ignota, 2019), *Futch journal* (2024), *Prototype* (2023), *Modron* (2023) and *Docks* (2024). And thanks to those events who supported performances and experimentation: Nawr, Tactile Bosch, Ghost Jam, No Matter, Language is a Virus, Gestures, PoEx Santiago de Chile, Poetics in Commons, Poetry Connections and Literature Across Frontiers, Indian Institute of Science Bengaluru, 1 Shanthi Road Bengaluru, Goran Spring Croatia, Poetry in Expanded Translation symposia, Luna de Locos Colombia, among others.

I'd also like to thank those who helped me edit *Poetry Wales* and co-curate Poetry Emergency festivals; many of the works we assembled inspired and nourished this poetry.

Lastly and crucially, for their support in many different forms, thank you to my partner, family, friends and to the poets, performers and teachers who assisted me in this work.